MOVING UP WITH SCIENCE

LIGHT

Peter Riley

W

To my granddaughter, Holly Jane.

Franklin Watts
Published in Great Britain in 2016 by The Watts Publishing Group

Editor: Hayley Fairhead
Designer: Elaine Wilkinson

ISBN: 978 1 4451 3519 9
Dewey classification number: 535

Printed in China

Franklin Watts
An imprint of Hachette Children's Group
Part of The Watts Publishing Group
Carmelite House, 50 Victoria Embankment, London EC4Y 0DZ

An Hachette UK Company
www.hachette.co.uk
www.franklinwatts.co.uk

Photo acknowledgements: brednikov p22 and p31b; catiamadio p6b and p30; Andy Crawford p8, p9b; Gergana Gevgalova p14 and p29; gmutlu p7; Gnomeandi p24; Aleksandar Hubenov p26b; Kwasny221 p18 and p31t; Rui Matos p15l; Ray Moller p20, p21t, p21b, p24b, p25t, p25bl; NASA p4; Maik Schrödter p6t and p28; Senior Master Sgt. George Thompson NASA p5; Yurchyk p15r; Peter Zijlstra p9t.

Artwork: John Alston

All other photographs by Leon Hargreaves.
With thanks to our models Sebastian Smith-Beatty, Florence Bursell and Sofia Bottomley.

Contents

Words in **bold** can be found in the glossary on pages 28–29.

Lights in the sky

If you look up into a clear night sky you will see **stars**. Do you know what they are made of?

Squashed gases

Stars are made of two **gases**. One is called helium. We use helium in party balloons to make them float in the air. The other gas is called hydrogen. The two gases squash together and make a huge **globe** of gas we call a star. At the centre of the star the squashed gases make light which shines out across space.

Stars shine with different colours of light. They can be blue, white, yellow, orange or red.

The Sun

The closest star to Earth is a yellow star. We call it the Sun. You must never look directly at the Sun, even if you are wearing sunglasses, as its bright light can harm your eyes.

Stars are **light sources** but there are other lights in the sky that are not light sources. They are the Moon and the **planets**.

The Moon shines with light that is **reflected** from the Sun.

Stars twinkle but planets shine steadily. Look in the night sky to see if you can find a planet among the stars.

What else makes light?

Stars are light sources out in space, but there are many things on Earth that make light too.

Fire and flames

When something burns it breaks up in the heat. Tiny **particles** rise up into the air. They are so hot they shine and make a flame. The tiny particles of **wax** from a burning candle make a flame which gives us light.

Tiny particles of burning wood make the flames above a bonfire.

Electric light sources

Electricity is used to make light in many objects we use in the home. Televisions, computers and mobile phones all have screens which light up when electricity passes through them. **LEDs** are tiny light sources which do not give out much heat when they light up. They are used for standby lights on televisions and as the numbers on electric clocks.

LEDs are used in Christmas lights.

Light bulbs

Some light bulbs have a thin wire **filament**. When electricity flows through it the wire gets so hot it gives out light. Some light bulbs have a coating on the inside which shines when electricity passes through the bulb. They are called low-energy light bulbs because they use less electricity than filament bulbs.

Low-energy light bulbs use less electricity than filament bulbs so they last much longer.

How many light sources can you find in your home?

Light and materials

Light moves very, very, fast. If you jump forwards by a metre it takes about a second. In that time light can travel three hundred million metres. In eight minutes light travels 150 million kilometres from the Sun to Earth!

How light moves

You can find out more about how light moves with this simple experiment. Put a card with a slit in it in front of a piece of dark coloured card, then shine a torch through the other side. You will see how the light travels in a straight line. This line of light is called a light ray. Because light moves so quickly, the light rays from the torch do not take long to reach the card.

Transparent, translucent and opaque

When light rays reach a **transparent** material they go straight through them. Glass, clear plastic and water are transparent materials.

When light rays reach a **translucent** material they scatter and some do not pass through. Tissue paper and frosted glass are translucent materials.

When light rays reach an **opaque** material they cannot pass through and some are reflected. Wood, brick and metal are opaque materials.

We cannot see the ice cream clearly because some light rays do not pass through the frosted glass.

We can see these sweets clearly because the light rays go straight through the clear glass jar.

This experiment shows that a book is opaque. Light rays can shine on one orange but cannot pass through the book, so the other orange is in the dark.

Dull, bright and shiny

When light rays strike an opaque material some are reflected, but others are **absorbed** or taken into the material. If a lot of light rays are absorbed the material looks dull. If fewer light rays are absorbed the material looks brighter.

The black paint is dull because it absorbs most of the light rays that strike it. The colour in the boy's T-shirt is bright because it absorbs fewer light rays.

Reflection of light rays

When you touch a material you touch its surface. The surface might be rough like wool or smooth like glass. When light rays travel towards a material they move in **parallel** lines.

If light rays are reflected from a very smooth material they keep travelling together in parallel lines. This makes the material shine. If they are reflected from a rough surface they move away in all directions.

When the girl shines a torch at this material it does not shine. You cannot see a picture called a reflection in the material's surface.

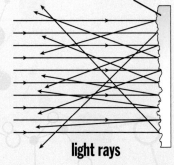

rough surface

light rays

When the girl shines the torch at a shiny plate, the torch's reflection can be seen in the plate.

smooth surface

light rays

A mirror

A mirror is made from a thin sheet of bright metal and a piece of glass. The bright metal is placed on the back of the glass.

Images

Nearly all the light on a mirror is reflected because its surface is bright and smooth. When you look in a mirror light rays from your face go to the surface of the mirror, creating a picture. All pictures you see in a mirror are called **images**.

The picture in the mirror appears because light rays are reflected by the mirror's smooth surface.

A picture in reverse

When you look at the top of your head in your mirror image it is in the same place as the top of your real head. When you look at your chin in your image it is in the same place as your real chin. But when you touch your right cheek with your hand, something different happens. Your image touches its left cheek. This switch is due to the way the light reflects. The image is **reversed**.

When you look in the mirror everything on the right goes to the left and everything on the left goes to the right.

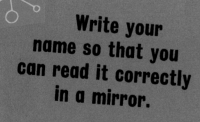

Write your name so that you can read it correctly in a mirror.

Darkness and light

The Earth gets light from the Sun. The Earth spins round in space like a slow-moving spinning top. As it turns only half the Earth is ever in sunlight. It is daytime there. The other half is in darkness. It is night-time there.

Dawn and dusk

When a place on the Earth turns towards the Sun and the sky becomes lighter we say that it is dawn. This is the time before sunrise. When a place turns away from the Sun and the sky becomes darker we say that it is dusk. This is the time after sunset.

When it is lunchtime on one side of the Earth it is the middle of the night on the other side.

Light at night

At night we may see by moonlight. The Sun shines onto the Moon. The Moon reflects the light like a mirror onto the dark side of the Earth. Most of our light at night comes from electric lights. Stars fill the night sky but are not bright enough for us to see by.

light rays

Moon

reflection of light rays

Earth

The Sun's light rays are reflected by the Moon onto the Earth.

Seeing in the light and dark

Light goes into our eyes through the black holes in their centres. These holes are called pupils. When it is light our pupils are small, but when it is dark our pupils get bigger. They do this to let more light in so that we can see better.

? How do your surroundings change after sunset? What can you see as it gets darker at dusk?

Dark and light test

Equipment:
• cardboard box with lid
• toy • tissue
• scissors • sticky tape

When scientists make a discovery they always want to find out more. They ask questions about their discovery and plan investigations to answer them. You can find out more about darkness and light with this experiment.

1.
Find a cardboard box. Ask an adult to cut a hole in one end of the box and cut out one end of the lid.

2.
Put a toy inside the box.

3.
Stick tissue paper over the top of the box to hide the toy.

4.
Place the lid on the box and ask a friend to look through the hole.

5.
Your friend should not be able to see anything because it is dark in the box. Now slowly slide the lid of the box to let more light in. Your friend should see more of the toy as more light enters the box.

Try this test with toys that are dull, bright or shiny. Do you get different results?

Shadows

Imagine you are in the woodland below. The Sun is behind the trees. Light rays travel from the Sun in all directions. When they reach the woodland floor and the trees, they are reflected up into your eyes. This lets you see the trees and the woodland floor.

Blocked light rays

The trees are opaque. They block the path of the light rays from the Sun, creating long, dark shapes on the woodland floor. These shapes are called **shadows**.

The shadows on the woodland floor are dark because light cannot pass through the trees.

How shadows form

Look at the shadows of the tree trunks. Each shadow has sharp dark lines that mark its edges. These sharp edges are due to the way light rays travel from a distant light source like the Sun. They move in straight parallel lines.

When light rays reach the edge of an opaque object, some are blocked and make a shadow. The light rays that have not been blocked pass over the edge of the object and make a sharp line.

If light rays did not travel in straight lines but bent from side-to-side, the edges of the shadows would be blurred or hazy.

light rays

shadow

opaque object

When you look at your shadow how is it different from looking at your image in a mirror?

The length of shadows

We have discovered how shadows are made (see pages 18–19).
We know that light comes from a source and that opaque
objects block light rays and make shadows.
But can we change the length
of a shadow?

Here is an experiment to investigate
the length of shadows and how
they change.

1.

Shine a torch
on a toy and ask a
friend to measure
the toy's shadow.

20

2.
Hold the torch higher and ask your friend to measure the length of the shadow again.

3.
Hold the torch lower and ask your friend to measure the length of the shadow again.

Does the length of the shadow change when the torch is held at different points? Explain your answer.

Shadows and time

The Earth is turning all the time. It takes 24 hours, or one day, for the Earth to make a complete turn.

The path of the Sun

When a place comes from the dark into the sunlight we say it is dawn in that place. The Sun appears to rise over the **horizon** in the east. All morning the Sun seems to rise in the sky until midday. In the afternoon it starts to sink in the sky. At sunset the Sun dips below the horizon in the west.

East

West

Changing shadows

As the Sun moves across the sky, shadows of opaque objects form on the ground. They change position as the Sun moves from east to west. When the Sun is in the east the shadows point to the west. When the Sun is in the west the shadows point to the east.

Make a shadow clock

This change in shadows can be used to measure time. You can make a shadow clock by placing a pencil in a ball of modelling clay on a piece of white paper, as shown.

Find out how it measures time by setting it up in a sunny place and marking the time and its shadow position every hour on a sunny day (see box below).

Before clocks and watches were invented, a shadow clock called a sundial was used to tell the time.

Use your shadow clock to measure time on different sunny days over two weeks. Always place the clock in the same position and use the same piece of paper you used on the first day. Is your shadow clock still accurate after two weeks?

Shadow shapes

Equipment:
- large piece of paper
- pen • a sunny day!

The height of a light source affects the length of a shadow. Does the height of the light source also affect the shadow shape?

1. Go outside on a sunny morning and look at your shadow as you stand on a large piece of white paper. Look at the size and shape of your head, arms and legs.

2. Ask a friend to draw around the edge of your shadow on the paper.

3. Go outside on a sunny lunchtime and stand exactly as you did in the morning. Look at the size and shape of your head, arms and legs again.

4. Ask a friend to draw around the edge of your shadow again.

During the morning your shadow will be much longer than it will be at lunchtime.

24

Direction of the light source

As you look at your shadow shape when the Sun is high in the sky, you will see that your shadow is much shorter than it was in the morning.

Try the following experiment to see how the direction of the light source also affects shadow shape.

Shine a light source on an object from lots of different directions and look at the many different shadow shapes you can make.

Try shining a torch on a range of different-shaped objects, such as beakers, cups with handles or toys. Shine the torch from lots of directions. Do the shadow shapes change?

Shadow size

You can make a very simple shadow puppet theatre by shining a light source on a wall and placing the puppets in front of the light source.

This shadow theatre is made by shining a light source on the back of a translucent screen. The puppets are placed between the light source and the screen.

Shadow puppets

You could try making your own shadow puppets using pieces of card and short sticks, such as lollipop sticks. Here are some puppets you could make and the shadows they will create on the wall.

Large and small shadows

What happens to the shadow if you move an object away from a light source? What happens to the shadow if you move an object towards a light source? You can use a pen and electric lamp to help you answer this question.

Distance from the light

If you move the object away from the light the shadow gets smaller. If you move the object towards the light the shadow gets larger.

Glossary

Absorb to take in. A sponge absorbs water. A dull material absorbs light rays.

Electricity a form of energy made by batteries and power stations, which travels along wires and makes lamps light, motors work and speakers make a sound.

Filament a very long, thin thread. In a light bulb it is made into a coiled wire.

Gas a substance which does not have any shape and can spread out in the air.

Globe a sphere.

Horizon the place in the distance where the sky and the land or sea meet. The horizon on land may have buildings or trees on it. The horizon looking out to sea will be flat or slightly curved.

Image the picture you see in a mirror.

LED Light Emitting Diode. It uses a small amount of electricity to give out light.

Light source something which gives out light.

Opaque the property of a material that does not let light pass through it.

Parallel rays or lines that run side-by-side at the same distance all the time.

Particle a very, very small piece of a solid material.

Planet a large spherical object made from rock or gases that moves around a star.

Reflect to bounce light off the surface of an object.

Reverse to turn round the other way.

Shadow a dark shape made on one side of an opaque object when light is shining onto the other side.

Star a huge ball of gases that gives out heat and light.

Translucent the property of a material which lets some light pass through it but scatters the rays in all directions.

Transparent the property of a material which lets light pass through it without being scattered.

Twinkle a quick change in brightness of stars due to the way the air moves above our heads.

Wax a solid material made from oil. Some wax is made by bees.

Answers to the activities and questions

Page 5 Lights in the sky

Activity: Most stars will appear white but you may see a few that are slightly blue, red, or orange. There may be one, two or three planets in the sky at one time that are easy to see. They are Jupiter, Venus and Mars. Mars has a slight red colour due to the sand on its surface.

Page 7 What else makes light?

Activity: This will depend on your home. You might like to group them room-by-room or according to whether they are lamps, screens or LEDS.

Page 13 A mirror

Activity: You may have to try for some time before you can draw something by looking at your drawing in the mirror. You need to reverse the shape of the letters for them to appear correctly in a mirror.

Page 15 Darkness and light

Answer: As the light fades, colours will become more difficult to see, until only black and shades of grey can be seen.

Page 17 Dark and light test

Activity: You may find that you have to slide the lid off more to see dull materials and slide it off less to see bright materials. You may have to slide the lid off even less to see shiny materials.

Page 19 Shadows

Answer: You can see parts of your face and their colours in a mirror. You cannot see parts of your face in a shadow. Your shadow can be tall or short, depending on the position of the light source.

Page 21 The length of shadows

Answer: Yes, the length of the shadow changes. It is longer when the torch is held lower. The light shines on a larger part of the object when it is low down and this makes the shadow longer.

Page 23 Shadows and time

Activity: If you use it to tell the time the following day you may find that it works quite well. If you use it to tell the time after a week or more you will find it does not work quite as well because the Sun's path across the sky may have changed slightly.

Page 25 Shadow shapes

Activity: If the object is a beaker without a handle it will stay the same but if it has a handle it will change when the light shines on the handle. Try a range of toys and see which one makes the highest number of different shadows.

Index

About this book

Moving Up with Science is designed to help children develop the following skills:

Science enquiry skills: researching using secondary sources, all pages; grouping and classifying, pages 5 and 7; observing over time, page 23; make comparative or fair test, pages 13, 17, 21, 25 and 27; pattern seeking, pages 17 and 25.

Working scientifically skills: making careful observations, pages 5 and 25; setting up simple practical enquiries, pages 7 and 25; make comparative or fair test, pages 17, 21, 23, 25 and 27; making accurate measurements, page 21; using results to draw simple conclusions, pages 7, 13, 17, 25 and 27; using straightforward scientific evidence to answer questions, pages 19 and 27.

Critical thinking skills: comprehension, page 15; analysis, pages 19 and 21.